LOCATION: _____ DATE: _____.

Your Eki Stamp Book is a great place to record your adventures across Japan. Stamps can be found at train stations, of course, but also at municipal buildings, cultural points and tourist attractions.

If you aren't sure if a location has a stamp, simply ask either:

"Eki sutanpu wa arimasu ka?" – "Do you have a station stamp?" if you are at a train station.

"Kinen sutanpu wa arimasu ka?" – "Do you have a commemorative stamp?" if you are at another location.

If you know a location has a stamp, ask either:

"Eki sutanpu wa doko desu ka?" – "Where is the station stamp?" if you are at a train station.

"Kinen sutanpu wa doko desu ka?" – "Where is the commemorative stamp?" if you are at another location.

The photo on the front of this stamp book is of the Hachikō statue located near Shibuya station, where the loyal Akita dog Hachikō waited for his deceased owner's return every day for almost a decade. This spot is not far from the Shibuya Scramble, the busiest intersection in the world. I took this pic back in 2017.

Each page in this stamp collection book is watermarked with a classic haiku from Matsuo Bashō, one of Japan's most famous poets. He lived during the Edo period, and Bashō is actually a pen name, taken after he received a Bashō tree and began to admire its resilience. He is considered the foremost master of the haiku form. His poems are often reproduced on monuments and traditional sites.

Image of Matsuo Bashō, courtesy of the Creative Commons.

LOCATION: _____ DATE: _____.

LOCATION: _____ DATE: _____.

LOCATION: _____ DATE: _____.

LOCATION: _____ DATE: _____.

LOCATION: _____ DATE: _____.

LOCATION: _____ DATE: _____.

LOCATION: _____ DATE: _____.

LOCATION: _____ DATE: _____.

LOCATION: _____ DATE: _____.

LOCATION: _____ DATE: _____.

LOCATION: _____ DATE: _____.

LOCATION: _____ DATE: _____.

LOCATION: _____ DATE: _____.

LOCATION: _____ DATE: _____.

LOCATION: _____ DATE: _____.

LOCATION: _____ DATE: _____.

LOCATION: _____ DATE: _____.

LOCATION: _____ DATE: _____.

LOCATION: _____ DATE: _____.

LOCATION: _____ DATE: _____.

LOCATION: _____ DATE: _____.

LOCATION: _____ DATE: _____.

LOCATION: _____ DATE: _____.

LOCATION: _____ DATE: _____.

LOCATION: _____ DATE: _____.

LOCATION: _____ DATE: _____.

LOCATION: _____ DATE: _____.

LOCATION: _____ DATE: _____.

LOCATION: _____ DATE: _____.

LOCATION: _____ DATE: _____.

LOCATION: _____ DATE: _____.

LOCATION: _____ DATE: _____.

LOCATION: _____ DATE: _____.

LOCATION: _____ DATE: _____.

LOCATION: _____ DATE: _____.

LOCATION: _____ DATE: _____.

LOCATION: _____ DATE: _____.

LOCATION: _____ DATE: _____.

LOCATION: _____ DATE: _____.

LOCATION: _____ DATE: _____.

LOCATION: _____ DATE: _____.

LOCATION: _____ DATE: _____.

LOCATION: _____ DATE: _____.

LOCATION: _____ DATE: _____.

LOCATION: _____ DATE: _____.

LOCATION: _____ DATE: _____.

LOCATION: _____ DATE: _____.

LOCATION: _____ DATE: _____.

LOCATION: _____ DATE: _____.

LOCATION: _____ DATE: _____.

LOCATION: _____ DATE: _____.

LOCATION: _____ DATE: _____.

LOCATION: _____ DATE: _____.

LOCATION: _____ DATE: _____.

LOCATION: _____ DATE: _____.

LOCATION: _____ DATE: _____.

LOCATION: _____ DATE: _____.

LOCATION: _____ DATE: _____.

LOCATION: _____ DATE: _____.

LOCATION: _____ DATE: _____.

LOCATION: _____ DATE: _____.

LOCATION: _____ DATE: _____.

LOCATION: _____ DATE: _____.

LOCATION: _____ DATE: _____.

LOCATION: _____ DATE: _____.

LOCATION: _____ DATE: _____.

LOCATION: _____ DATE: _____.

LOCATION: _____ DATE: _____.

LOCATION: _____ DATE: _____.

LOCATION: _____ DATE: _____.

LOCATION: _____ DATE: _____.

LOCATION: _____ DATE: _____.

LOCATION: _____ DATE: _____.

LOCATION: _____ DATE: _____.

LOCATION: _____ DATE: _____.

LOCATION: _____ DATE: _____.

www.ingramcontent.com/pod-product-compliance
Lightning Source LLC
Chambersburg PA
CBHW061804070526
44586CB00023B/2705